THE ISSUE OF THE COVENANTS

NYRON MEDINA

The Issue Of The Covenants

First Published 2017. First Written July, 1995

All inquiries should be addressed to:

Thusia Seventh Day Adventist Church

Romain Lands, Lady Young Road,

Morvant,

Trinidad and Tobago

Telephone#: 1-868-625-0446

www.thusiasdaevangel.com

Unless otherwise indicated, Scripture quotations are from the King James Version of the Bible.

ISBN-13: 978-1977538840

ISBN-10: 1977538843

Front Cover Illustration by Nyron Medina

"... Because this the covenant which I shall covenant to the house of Israel after the days those, is saying Lord, giving laws of me into the mental perception of them, and upon hearts of them I shall write upon them, and I shall be to them into God and they will be to me into people..." Hebrews 8:10 **(Greek)**

A Publication of Thusia Seventh Day Adventist Church

Printed in the United States of America

TABLE OF CONTENTS

PREFACE

The greatest Evangelical doctrine that seeks to undermine and destroy the Law of God and the Sabbath is the doctrine of the Covenants which is anti-nomian in its nature. This doctrine cannot be true because there are no scriptures in the Bible that present the Law or the Sabbath as abolished, nor is there any explaining love as a replacement of the Law. Thus, if the Law is to be kept and if Love **is** fulfilling the Law - concept that has always existed even in Old Testament (First Witness) times - then the anti-nomian doctrine of the covenants cannot be true.

It is equally so with the doctrine of Grace. No scripture presents Grace as a replacement of the Law (under the erroneous covenants teaching), the Old Testament (First Witness) specifically presents Grace as existing alongside Law; in fact, the Law itself is an expression of God's Grace.

This booklet, therefore, has proposed to present a doctrine of the covenants that is pro-nomian, or rather it leaves God's Law and the Sabbath intact. The things herein presented, attempt to show what was really taught in the Bible concerning the Old and New Covenants, a doctrine that embodies enforcement of God's Law. It is the hope of the author that the readers are greatly enlightened and use this teaching to destroy Evangelical anti-nomianism, which is destroying society and sending people to hell.

God bless you.

Nyron Medina

INTRODUCTION

Among the many controversies upon the earth today, one of them stands out as extremely important in that it is tied in with the claim of the validity of the Law of God. In a nutshell, the argument goes like this: **The old covenant is the Law; the new covenant is the Grace of God in Christ. With the death of Christ the old covenant - the Law was abolished, and the new covenant is now in force.** This tells us that the Law no longer has to be kept, or that the works of the Law are not necessary for salvation, also that we are saved by Grace without the works of the Law.

This is the general argument of many Sunday keeping churches today, to excuse their transgression of **YHWH's** Sabbath and to justify their honouring of Sunday.

Since they have no direct scripture that shows the Law to be abolished, all they have to do to get the Law out of the way is to claim that the Law was the old covenant, thus the law was abolished. But why that hate against God's Law, what is behind this anti-nomianism?

The answer is the Sabbath. Unsanctified emotions find the Sabbath unpalatable, and to rid of it they simply claim that the Sabbath is abolished; when requested to give Biblical proof, since there is none they resort to saying the Law was abolished, and because there are no scriptures to also ratify the "theory" that the Law was abolished, the claim that the Law is the old covenant and the old covenant was abolished is presented as the final court of appeal.

Thus anti-nomianism is anti-Sabbatarianism, and the idea of the covenants is both. So in brief the argument goes like this:

OLD COVENANT WOULD MEAN ⟶ LAW IS ABOLISHED⟶THUS SABBATH IS ABOLISHED.

This study is intended to totally repudiate this false concept. The pattern it follows would be an exposition of the real issue of the covenants as it is in the Bible, and a refutation of the anti-nomian idea of covenants as is presented in the writings of the "new" Worldwide Church of God.

THE MEANING OF THE WORD COVENANT

What does the word covenant mean? We start our search with the original Hebrew word so translated and then the Greek word in the Second Witness (New Testament).

The Hebrew word translated "covenant" is "b'rith", and the word is of doubtful meaning to many scholars whose conjectures differ as far as the east is from the west. But this one meaning seems to make the most sense.

"Thus Gesenius - Buhl derives "b'rith" from the root "baraya" as it is used in 1 Sam 17:8 (the word is translated "choose" in the KJV, meaning "to decide" or "allot to".

Those etymologies point toward the giving of an inheritance and favour the meaning "testament". J. Barton Payne, **The Theology of the Older Testament**, p. 79.

Here the Hebrew word "b'rith" translated "covenant" is presented as favouring the word "testament". This is the best we can go in the original meaning of the word which is obviously shrouded in mystery. But what of the word "testament", a word used often in the KJV (for example Revelation 11:19)? Observe the meaning:

"Testament, n. [From Latin "testameutum", from "testor," to make a will]. A solemn authentic instrument in writing by which a person declares his will as to the disposal of his estate and effects after his death: This is otherwise called a "will".

A testament, to be valid, must be made when the testator is of sound mind, and it must be subscribed, witnessed and published in such manner as the law prescribes. A man in certain cases may make a valid will by words only, and such will is called "nuncupative" Noah Webster, **An American Dictionary of the English Language (1828 edition)**.

We shall observe that this same meaning is the true understanding of the original words translated covenant. However, the Hebrew word "b'rith" being obscure, we can at least say this about it:

> *"Although there may at times appear certain mutually binding conditions so that we call the resultant arrangement a "covenant", these conditions do not represent the essence of the **"b'rith"**. It is still a sovereignly imposed, monopleuric injunction...Hence, God chooses the word **"b'rith"**, the available term for a legally binding instrument, to describe what is His sovereign pleasure.*

*When the parties concerned are God in grace and man in his sin, on whose behalf God acts, the **"b'rith"** becomes God's self-imposed obligation for the deliverance of sinners...It is not 'compact' or 'contract' or "agreement" that provides the constitutive or governing idea but that of "dispensation" in the sense of disposition...*

*Though essentially monergistic, effectuated by "one worker", (God, not man and God), the **b'rith** required that men qualify."* J. Barton Payne, **The Theology of the Older Testament**, p. 81.

A more positive way of finding out the real meaning of the Hebrew word **"b'rith"** is to understand the meaning of the Greek word with which it is translated.

If we can determine the true meaning of this word, we shall know from its use in the Septuagint (the Greek version of the First Witness or (Old Testament), and from the second witness or (New Testament) just what **"b'rith"** meant.

> *"In the New Testament the Greek word that represents "b'rith" is "diatheke". The primary meaning of "diatheke" is a "disposition of property by will"...Thus in the Septuagint, the pre-Christian Greek translation of the Old Testament, "diatheke" is employed to translate "b'rith" throughout".* **Ibi**d., pp. 82,83.

We have many testimonies that **"diatheke"** means a "will" from a broad spectrum of scholars:

*"**Diatheke** at the time when the septuagint and the New Testament came into existence not only could mean "testament", but such was the current meaning of the word…The legal usage, however, referring it to a testamentary disposition had monopolized the word…**"diatheke"** meant currently "last will"…"* Geerhadus Vos, **Biblical Theology**, p. 24.

*"**Diatheke…** in profane Greek always signifies the disposition which a person makes of his property in prospect of death, i.e. testament; this*

is its meaning when used either in the singular or plural…being the testamentary arrangements of a person." Hermann Cremer, **Biblico-Theological Lexicon of New Testament Greek**, p. 549.

Another thorough examination of the contemporary meaning of the Greek word **"diatheke"** yields the same definition:

> *"In papyri and inscriptions the word means **testament**, **will**, with absolute unanimity, and such frequency that illustration is superfluous...Against this word stands **suntheke** (not in NT),....It is to the last the word for **compact**, just as **"diatheke"** is always and only the word for will...*

> ***"diatheke"*** *is properly "dispositio", an "arrangement" made by one party with plenary power, which the other party may accept or reject, but cannot alter.*

*A will is simply the most conspicuous example of such an instrument ... A covenant offered by God to man was no "compact" between two parties coming together on equal terms. **"Diatheke"** in its primary sense, as described above, was exactly the needed word... Deissmann (St. Paul, p. 152) insists on **testament** everywhere...even a Jew like Paul, with Greek language in the very fibre of his thought, could never have used **"diatheke"** for **covenant** without the slightest consciousness of its ordinary and invariable contemporary meaning".* J.H. Moulton and G. Milligan, **The Vocabulary of the Greek Testament**, pp. 148,149.

Thus, we have positive proof for the meaning of the word **"b'rith"** in its namesake **"diatheke"**. Furthermore, the following should be considered.

> *"...no one in the Mediterranean world in the first century A.D. would have thought of finding in the word **"diatheke"** the idea of "covenant". St. Paul would not, and in fact did not".* A. Deissmann, **Light from the Ancient East**, p. 337.

So the idea of "an agreement between two persons" as the meaning of the word covenant was not what was meant by the words **"b'rith"** and **"diatheke"**, this meaning is foreign to the Bible-writers. The word "will" or "testament" was what was meant by the words.

*"The Greek translators, however, seem deliberately to have avoided representing **"b'rith"** by the word **"suntheke"**, which is the ordinary term for a compact or mutual agreement. **"Suntheke"** means literally a thing "put together" and its connotations of legal equality rendered it inappropriate for application to the revealed will of the sovereign God. **"Diatheke",** a thing "put through" was thus assigned to **"b'rith"** and was then used for all occurrences of the Hebrew word even when it described a human agreement. **"Diatheke"** had become a comprehensive term…*

> *The conclusion is this: Wherever* ***"diatheke"*** *occurs in the New Testament, it means just one thing, "testament".* J. Barton Payne, **The Theology of the Older Testament**, pp. 83,85.

It is now time that we look into the Bible itself to gain a real understanding of the meaning of the word **"diatheke"** by the nature of its use.

THE BIBLICAL USAGE

There are many places in the Bible where the Word "covenant" is used, but its uses are not enough to give an explanation of what it is all about, we do not get an explanation of the real meaning of the word in the form of a definition. However, there is one place in the Bible where sufficient explanation of what is involved in a **"diatheke"** is given, and from that we can gain a real understanding of the meaning of the word and thus understand the word "covenant" differently. This place is Hebrews 9:15-20. In the KJV the word **"diatheke"** is translated "testament" (which means will) because this is found to be the natural meaning.

We are not attempting an interpretation of the text, but our primary effort is to call attention to how the word is used in these verses. In Hebrews 9:15 we see that Christ in His mediatory role makes us receive the "eternal inheritances", His death qualified Him to purchase us out of the bondage of sin and release us free (that is, in obedience).

See Romans 3:24; Romans 6:12,13,17,18. Even past transgressions are dealt with by Christ on the grounds of His eternal suffrage (Revelation 13:8). But Hebrews 9:15 tells us that Christ is the "mediator of the new testament ..." What is this new testament"? It is in Hebrews 8:8-12 and the word **"diatheke"** is there translated "covenant". The "testament" or "will" God has made with man is a means of saving man from sin, a subjective work done only by His Spirit. This is exactly what is presented in Hebrews 9:14, the "... purge your conscience from dead works to serve the living God".

In Hebrews 9:16 we are told the fact about a "will" or "testament", that the will maker is expecting to die so that he makes a will, that is, a testimony, of what he intends to give to the one whom he is blessing. So we can understand that Christ was supposed to die, (John 10:10,11,15), so He testified what He intended to give us through His death; the content of Hebrews 8:8-12 is it. Hebrews 9:14 reinforces this.

Hebrews 9:17 tells us that it is death that bequeaths to us what is in a "will" or "testament", so that nothing is bequeathed while the will maker is yet alive.

Upon His death Christ testified of what we were to get, it is in Hebrews 8:8-12, that is the content of His will, and the influence of Christ's death speaks this to us and it is given when we repent and believe (Mark 1:15), by the resurrected Christ in the heavenly sanctuary (Hebrews 8:1-7).

Could you imagine fitting the wrong idea of covenant into these verses? If a covenant was indeed an agreement between two persons, the two persons needed to be alive to cut it, none of the parties need to die to make it.

In fact death would nullify any agreement that had been previously made and carried out while both parties or at least one was yet alive. Death therefore, destroys this type of covenant so that the idea cannot fit into Hebrews 9:16,17, but one can readily understand a will or testament as explained in the verses.

Hebrews 9:18-20 refers to the testament (or covenant) in the First Witness (OT) relating to verses 16 and 17, thus telling us that the whole use of the word **"b'rith"** in the First Witness in the Hebrew and **"diatheke"** in the Septuagint should also mean "will" or "testament".

The death of the animal meant death had occurred and that a bequeathal was being given to Israel, a ceremonial system pointing to Christ (Galatians 3:24). Thus the natural God-intended meaning for the word was "will" or "testament".

THE SENSE OF WILL OR TESTAMENT

But how can we understand will or testament? The basic thing to understand is what the disposition of the will-maker - in this sense God - was all about. What does the document of a will or testament show about God's disposition or mind? God's intention must be understood, and the content of His will must be also understood, however, the latter is an indication to the former.

From the content of the will in Hebrews 8:8-12, we draw the testimony that God has Love to us, not just Love, but salvific Love, a Love that efficiently deals with man's problem of sin. This reminds us of John 3:16; Romans 5:8,9; 1 John 3:16.

In reality a document of a will, or whatever way a will is made, it is essentially a testimony of God's sincere heart-intention of salvific Love towards sinners.The will is a testimony and gift expressing how God thinks towards us. We see thoughts of Love to the point of giving Himself for our salvation (Matthew 1:23).

So we can understand "new covenant" or "testament" as "new testimony and gift of God's Love towards us". And is this not what Christ gave? A new testimony and gift of God's Love towards us! This is very important and has many implications for our understanding the issue of the covenants.

APPLICATIONS TO COVENANT ISSUE

In applying what we just understood to the fact of the old and new covenants or testament, many misconceptions in the camp of the Evangelicals are exposed. For example: since covenant is testament, and it means a will or a testimony of God's heart towards humanity in sin, as salvation is from the beginning (see Hebrews 11), then God must have had a salvific heart of Love towards sinners then. So the old covenant or testament would not be an old way of salvation (and there is only one way Acts 4:10-12), of this saving Love, one that has now become obsolete and is replaced with the incarnation, doing and death of Jesus.

In this way Jesus is become the mediator (or influence dispenser) of the new testimony of God's heart of salvific Love to sinners, not a new replacement of an old Law-based way of salvation. The difference is crucial, because one point shows a change of testimony formation while the other claims a change in an old way of salvation, that is, by the works of the Law.

But salvation was **never** by the works of the Law not in Abraham's time nor from Moses to Jesus, it was always by God's effectual spiritual working upon our hearts (Psalm 51:10,17), it was always through the Grace of God who at that time also put the Law in the hearts of the First Witness (OT) people (Psalm 37:30,31). The content of God's will or testament has never changed, they are still the same today. It is the type of testimony for those same contents that has changed. This must be carefully seen.

What we are saying in effect is that the way God has shown His eternal salvific Love- through the Ceremonial system- that has changed; it is the old covenant or testimony of God's Love. The incarnation, doing and dying of Jesus this is the new testimony of God's undying Love. Is testimony or will content also?

Yes, it is moreso. The content of the old testament (or covenant) was the ceremonial system which also testified of God's salvific Love, the content of the new testament (or covenant) is the incarnation, doing and dying of Jesus which gives a "better" testimony of God's salvific Love. What we next need to understand is the issue of "new" covenant. What is "new"? And why "new" covenant or testament?

WHAT "NEW" MEANS

Of all the places in the Bible where the word "new" is used associated with covenant or testament the majority word for new is the Greek **"kainos"**. Only in one instance another Greek word for new - **"neos"** - is used, and that is in Hebrews 12:24. But in Matthew 26:28; Mark 14:24; Luke 22:20; 1 Corinthians 11:25; 2 Corinthians 3:6; Hebrews 8:8,13 and Hebrews 9:15 it is **"kainos"**.

In Hebrews 10:20 where we are told of a "new and living way" the word for "new" in that verse is **"prosphatos"** which is synonymous to **"kainos"** so in understanding that word "Kainos" we shall cover **"prosphatos"**.

The facts are that the two Greek words translated "new" - **"kainos"** and **"neos"** have different meanings, they mean new in different senses. Of the word **"neos"** we are told:

> *"Contemplate the new under aspects of **time**, as that which has recently come into existence and this is **neos"**.* Richard C. Trench, **Synonyms of the New Testament**, pp. 219-220.

> *"**Neos** traditionally focuses on time. The thing it describes is "new" in the sense of being newly arrived, or just appearing. Thus **neos** wine is this year's crop".* Lawrence O. Richards, **Expository Dictionary of the Bible Words**, p. 458.

"New, recent. New in relation to time, that which has recently come into existence or become present". Spiros Zodhiates, **The Complete Word Study Dictionary New Testament**, p. 1007.

But of the word "kainos" we are also told:

*"New in the aspect of quality is **kainos** ..."* **Ibid**., p. 1007.

"New, i.e., current or not before known, newly introduced." **Ibid**., p. 804.

*"The classical word that indicates new (and superior) in quality is **kainos.** In secular Greek usage the **kainos** was definitely better than the old...*

"new" in the qualitative sense..." Lawrence O. Richards, **Expository Dictionary of Bible Words**, p. 458.

*"But contemplate the new, not now under aspects of **time**, but of **quality**, the new, as set over against that which has seen service, the outworn, the effete or marred through age, and this is **kainos**... **kainos** will often, as a secondary notion, imply praise; for the new is commonly better than the old... **kainos**... implies that it is something not only new but sufficiently diverse from what had gone before..."* Richard C. Trench, **Synonyms of the New Testament**, pp. 220,221,222.

Thus the evidence of the real meaning of the two Greek words for "new" - **"neos"**, and **"kainos"** could be summed up as:

a. **Neos**- new as to **time**, that is, now present in time.

b. **Kainos**- new as to **quality**, superior, but not as to time.

Now how do we judge the fact that only one text - Hebrews 12:24 - uses the word "neos" with covenant, while eight scriptures, all the remaining texts with covenant, have **"kainos"** in them?

THE NEOS COVENANT

The text is in fact easy to understand; in it we are told that "Jesus (is) the mediator of the new (**neos**) covenant..." We have already understood that the word "covenant" is not the appropriate word, the better word is "will" or "testament", so that the text should read: "...Jesus (is) the mediator of the new will/testament..."

When we consider that the Will contains the inness of the Law with regards to the human heart, and our service to God (Hebrews 8:8-13; Hebrews 10:16,17), and also the incarnation, doing and dying of Jesus (Hebrews 12:24; 1 Corinthians 11:23-26; Romans 11:26,27; Hebrews 10:29), we have to ask what about these things are new (neos) as to time?

The answer is certainly the incarnation, doing and dying of Jesus Christ. These things are new, having never occurred in time before, and this is the context of the use of "new covenant" in Hebrews 12:24.

But as to the Law in the heart which is also in the new will (covenant), this part is not new in the sense of now come, this has always been the only way of salvation.

Observe how this new covenant/will has the "blood of sprinkling..." (Hebrews 12:24), "...blood of the covenant (will)... "(Hebrews 10:29), and is called the "...blood of the everlasting covenant..." (Hebrews 13:20). It is new (**neos**) yet "everlasting".

This is because in Hebrews 12:24, the blood of Christ part of the content of the Will/covenant, is new (**neos**), but not the work of the changing of the heart and perfecting of the works (Hebrews 13:21), a result of the "blood of Christ" is not new or now come.

So we have here the will or covenant of God in which some of its contents are of recent historical transactions, or new as **neos**, and we have some as everlasting realities. For example:

WILL/COVENANT

A. Incarnation

B. Earthly life of Jesus

C. Death/Blood of Jesus

D. Resurrection of Jesus (Kainos things)

E. Law in heart

F. God being our God, we being his people

G. Forgiveness of sins/Justification etc.

But what about the part of the Will/Covenant that is called **"kainos"**?

THE KAINOS COVENANT

All the remaining texts that have "new covenant/testament" have the word **"kainos"**. They are Matthew 26:28; Mark 14:24; Luke 22:20; 1 Corinthians 11:25; 2 Corinthians 3:6; Hebrews 8:8,13 and Hebrews 9:15. The number of texts is eight **"kainos"** compared to only one **"neos"**. The consensus certainly is in favour of **kainos** will/covenant".

This is not the now come things, but everlasting things, qualitative things or superior things. So that the "new covenant/testament" speaks about the things that are qualitatively better than the "old covenant". So the phrase "new (**kainos**) covenant/testament" simply means a "fresh", "restated", "better", "superior" covenant/testament, not a now come as to time covenant.

Thus the content of the covenant/will in Hebrews 8:8-12, has been existing in the time of the First Witness (OT). Take for instance the phrase "...I will be to them a God and they shall be to me a people..." Hebrews 8:10. This phrase is a direct quote from Genesis 17:7, which explains the covenant/Will that God made with Abraham.

The same phrase is also found in a number of scriptures among which we have Leviticus 26:12; Ezekiel 28:26; Jeremiah 24:7; Jeremiah 31:1; Jeremiah 32:38; Ezekiel 11:20; Ezekiel 36:28; Ezekiel 37:27; Hosea 2:23; Zechariah 8:8 and Zechariah 13:9. This clearly shows that the contents of the new (**kainos**) will/covenant, is not new (**neos**), now come with the death of Christ, but was in force as the only way of salvation long before the historical death of Jesus. It was the covenant God made with Abraham (Genesis 17:7) and his seed in which **anyone** who is to ever be saved must share in (Galatians 3:16,29).

Thus we see clearly that there is only **one way** of salvation from Adam to the end of the world, and God introduced no type of "covenant" that ever interfered with the promises made in the everlasting will/covenant (Galatians 3:17,18). What have we thus learned from all this?

SUMMARY

In summary, we understand that "covenant" should be "will" or "testament", and that new (**neos**) identified parts of the everlasting covenant that came later, such as the incarnation, doing and dying of Jesus, while **"kainos"** (new) identifies the parts of the covenant that have always been intact, but presents them as qualitatively better or superior. Also the incarnation, doing and dying of Jesus is also qualitatively better though they are new (neos) now come.

So the new covenant/testament/will is in fact God's attitude or disposition of salvific Love towards us as testified in the incarnation, doing and dying of Jesus (John 3:16).

A special thing must be noted with regards to the Law and its center-the Sabbath. We are to be judged by all of this Law of ten commandments (James 2:8-12), in the "new" "kainos" (qualitatively better) covenant/testament/will, the Law is to be placed in our hearts just as it had been done in the First Witness (OT). (Hebrews 8:10; Hebrews 10:16; Psalm 37:30,31).

Now if this Law, with its Sabbath, had been abolished as a part of the old covenant, then no one should be justified by it, neither should it be put in the heart of anyone. And if one were to say that Love is the new commandment, then that new is not **"neos"**/now come, but **"kainos"**/qualitatively better or superior, and the scriptures teach that Love is the fulfilling of the ten commandments (Romans 13:8-12; James 2:8,9). Love as the fulfilling of the Law was also the exact requirement of the worship of Yahweh in the First Witness (OT) (Leviticus 19:17,18,34; Deuteronomy 10:19).

When Jesus presented Love to God and Love to man as the real point of the first Witness (OT) and that it was applicable to Second Witness (NT) times (Mark 12:28-33), He showed that the true religion of Yahweh was always obedience to the Law (1 John 5:2,3). How then this could be abolished as the old covenant?

THE OLD COVENANT

What then is the old covenant? We have already understood that covenant is will or testament, thus the old covenant is the old will or testament. This means that there were requirements to be practiced to point men to sin's horribleness and to God (Galatians 3:19,24). These requirements were not what gave salvation, but pointed the way as a testimony of the Love of God.

In other words they pointed to the real everlasting covenant/testament or to the spiritual facts of salvation which were the real covenant. In the Second Witness (NT) **"old covenant"** is used to identify only the ceremonial system given to the Israelites. We do not find it touching the Law of Ten Commandments at all.

The ceremonial system was made up of holy days, rituals, and sacrificial requirements (Numbers 29).None of these things were meant to give salvation and to think so was to miss the whole point of them (Hebrews 10:1-4; Galatians 3:19,24). Texts in the Second Witness that in one way or another show that the ceremonial system was the old covenant are for example: Hebrews 7:11,12,16-19,28; Hebrews 8:4,7; Hebrews 9:1-7,12,13,18,21; Hebrews 10:1-9. **The term "old covenant" is frankly a Pauline term; it is not used by God**, but however the term "new/kainos" covenant would imply an "old" one as Paul shows us (Hebrews 8:13).

God tells us about only a "new/kainos" or qualitatively superior covenant/ testament (Hebrews 8:8,9), and from that Paul draws an implication of "old" covenant.

Now the Greek word for "old" in Hebrews 8:13 is **"palaios"**, and it means: "...old, that which has been around for a long time but not necessary from the beginning as the word **"archaios**" ... would imply, as being original." Spiros Zodhiates, **The Complete Word Study Dictionary**, **New Testament**, p. 805.

This finally clarifies the difference of new/**kainos**, and old/**palaios** covenants/testaments. While the new/**kainos** testament is the incarnation, doing and dying of Jesus, the Law being in the heart, and God being our God, and we being his people, and forgiveness of sins (Hebrews 8:10-12), the old/**palaios** and contrasted testament is the ceremonial system.

We are being told in the Bible that the Life of Christ and forgiveness of sins is a qualitatively better or superior will or testimony of God's Love, than rituals, holy days and sacrificial requirements which have been around for some time, but not from the beginning. That is all that is meant; but these Evangelical sects misrepresent the fact about the old covenant, when they present "old" as meaning the covenant written in the Old Testament (FW), just because the word "old" is used they look for the word "covenant" in the Old Testament (FW) and call what they find "old covenant". As they find that the Ten Commandments is called covenant in the Old Testament, and the Sabbath also, they call them the Old Covenant, and as the old covenant is abolished they connectively say that the Law and especially the Sabbath is abolished.

This is a most serious mistake; because, the Law and Sabbath are not the old covenant since it is the Law in the heart (which includes the Sabbath) that constitutes the new covenant/testament, and the meaning of the word "old" is merely that which has been around for a long time, but not from the beginning, and applies to the ceremonial system.

One must remember that the Law and Sabbath have been around not merely for a long time but from the very beginning (Genesis 2:1-3; Hebrews 4:3,4; Genesis 4:7), thus "palaios" does not apply to them. This brings us to the issue of the covenant in the First Witness (FW).

WHAT WAS THE COVENANT IN THE FIRST WITNESS

We can start with Abraham. Apart from God promising Abraham land and children (Genesis 12:7; Genesis 13:14-16; Genesis 15:5,18), in His will/testament, He promised true religion and all that it implied to Abraham and his seed (Genesis 17:7). But we see in Genesis 17 double covenants, one which is symbolical and one which is spiritual.

We will call them the symbolical covenant and the Spiritual Covenant for clarity and distinction. The real covenant is in Genesis 17:7, that is the Spiritual Covenant, the other one, the symbolical Covenant is the "seed" promised to Abraham in Genesis 17:8, the land of Canaan, Genesis 17:8, and circumcision in Genesis 17:10-14. Circumcision in Genesis 17:11 is even called a "token" which means a "sign" of the real covenant of Genesis 17:7.

Thus when God declared His covenant/testament to Abraham, it was double covenants/testaments God made. One was the **SPIRITUAL COVENANT** (called the new covenant in the Second Witness), and the other was the **SYMBOLICAL COVENANT** (called the old covenant in the Second Witness).

The Symbolical Covenant was a public testimony of the Spiritual Covenant something like baptism is a sign of the death of the old man of sin and the resurrection of the new man in Christ (Romans 6:3-7). The Symbolical Covenant was designed to testify of the Spiritual Covenant which was the salvific Love of God.

The fact that when God made or gave His Covenant to Abraham it was two covenants made at that time can be seen in the following examples.

1) (a) Seed of children promised to Abraham. Genesis 15:5,18.

(b) But this symbolized Christ. Galatians 3:16

2) (a) Land promised to Abraham. Genesis 15:18; Genesis 17:8

(b) This symbolizes the new earth and new Jerusalem. Romans 4:13; Hebrews 11:8-10,14-16.

3) (a) Circumcision was given. Genesis 17:10-14

(b) But it symbolized Righteousness by Faith. Romans 4:11

4) (a) Finally, when God said that in Abraham shall all the nations of the earth be blessed. Genesis 12:2,3.

(b) He meant the promise of the Spirit. Galatians 3:8,9,14.

This establishes beyond the shadow of doubt that whenever God made a covenant in the First Witness (OT), He really made double covenants. Thus we see that when God promised the tribe of Judah kingship in Israel, He spiritually meant Jesus, the Lion of the tribe of Judah. When He promised David that he will have seed ruling on the throne, He meant Jesus the Son of David as the true King. In every case the symbolical was an indication to the spiritual. Sometimes, the symbolical alone would be made, but behind it would be the spiritual; (as for example, nowhere did God promise the world to Abraham, only the land of Canaan, but in Romans 4:13 we see for the first time that Canaan symbolized the world). Sometimes the spiritual alone would be made, but there would be a symbolical to enforce the spiritual upon the consciousness.

The same case is true for the covenant/testament declared by God at Mt. Sinai. This covenant is explained in Exodus chapters 20-23, and in Exodus 24:1-8 it is ratified by animal blood. Certainly, God would not make a symbolical Covenant alone with all Israel as if that could save them, in Exodus 20-23, there must be a Spiritual Covenant in the Mt. Sinai event, a covenant by which the people are brought to "...love (God) and keep (His) commandments."

Exodus 20:6, so that they would be saved. Whosoever thinks that the Spiritual Covenant of Righteousness by Faith (which includes the Law in the heart etc.) were denied to Israel from Moses to Jesus have a terribly wrong understanding of Mt. Sinai. The giving of the Law was never meant to save, it could not have negated the covenant of the Spirit made by God to Abraham (Galatians 3:17,18), the giving of the Law at Mt. Sinai was not against the Spiritual Covenant-promises of God to Abraham.

(Galatians 3:21). Anyone to be saved was to be saved by the Spiritual Covenant promises made to Abraham as Abraham's seed and blessed with him (Galatians 3:6-9,14,16,29).

Salvation was always through the Faith of Jesus Christ from Adam to the end (Romans 4:16). Thus at Mt. Sinai, a Spiritual Covenant and a symbolical Covenant were made. That the real covenant made was Spiritual is seen in Jeremiah 7:21-23.

That the Ten Commandments was given as part of the Spiritual Covenant at Mt. Sinai is seen in the fact that it is Love from the heart that is the fulfilling of this law (Exodus 20:6). A major interpretation of the giving of the covenant at Sinai is found in the book of Deuteronomy. But aspects of the spirituality of the covenant at Sinai could be seen in Exodus itself.

For example, God being Israel's God as seen in the Spiritual covenant to Abraham in Genesis 17:7, is to be found in Exodus 25:8; Exodus 29:45,46 also in Exodus 34:6,7. But in the book of Deuteronomy, there are literally dozens of statements that show that the everlasting, new (**kainos**) and Spiritual Covenant was in fact made by God with Israel at Mt. Sinai. In Deuteronomy 4:13 we see the Law of the ten commandments is called God's covenant.

In Deuteronomy 4:19,23 Israel is forbidden from worshipping the sun, moon, stars or any graven image, if they do that they will forget the covenant of Yahweh their God; of course this is a heart matter and service to God here must be the Spiritual Covenant. In Deuteronomy 5:2 the fact that God made a covenant with Israel in Mt. Sinai is recounted, the ten commandments Law is repeated by Moses in Deuteronomy 5:6-21, verse 10 shows that it is heart Love that fulfills this Law, this is the Spiritual or **Kainos** Covenant.

In Deuteronomy 5:22 Moses shows that the law was limited to only ten precepts and no more, then Deuteronomy 5:29 it is wished that Israel would have the right "heart in them" to fear God and keep the Law, this is certainly an indication to the spirituality of the covenant.

In Deuteronomy 6:4,5,6 God's oneness is presented, also loving God with all one's heart (which is keeping His commandments John 14:15; 1 John 5:2,3) is presented, and the fact that the Law was to be put in Israel's heart is seen, and what is that but the new (**kainos**) covenant that is spiritual covenant, "our righteousness" is the works of the Law done by us through the Faith of God (Romans 3:31; Romans 2:26,27).

Deuteronomy 7:9 shows the covenant God keeping mercy with those that "...love him and keep his commandments...". Again this is the new/**kainos** covenant, because love is from the heart.

Deuteronomy 8:2,3,5,6 speaks about the Law with phrases like "...in thine heart...", "live by... every word...", "...consider in thine heart...", surely this is the **kainos**/new covenant.

Deuteronomy 10:4,5 recounts God writing the Law and Moses putting the tables of stone in the ark, and in Deuteronomy 10:12,13 Moses shows what the Lord requires of Israel with regards to this Law; we are told that they are to obey the Law with Love from their hearts for their good, this is indeed the Spiritual Covenant.

However, as we come to Deuteronomy 10:16-19, we are told how to cure the stiff-necked attitude of the people.

Their hearts were to be circumcised which is a renewing of the mind (Romans 2:28,29; Ephesians 4:23,24, Colossians 2:11,13), and they were commanded to love the stranger.

Surely this is the same Spiritual Covenant as is expressed in the Second Witness (NT) Even Deuteronomy 11:1 again calls for Israel to love God which is keeping His commandments (1 John.5:2,3). This same call is repeated in Deuteronomy 11:13 and 22, Deuteronomy 11:18 tells us the Law should be in their heart. All this is the **kainos**/new covenant.

Deuteronomy 19:9 repeats Love to God as Law keeping, the Spiritual Covenant. The fact that the Israelites were to be established as "an holy people" if they kept the Law as shown in Deuteronomy 28:9, how that they were not devoid of the saving Love of God of the better covenant though they were given the ceremonial system. Deuteronomy 30:2 shows heart obedience is necessary and in Deuteronomy 30:6 shows that God is the one to circumcise the heart to make the Israelites love Him and keep His Law, isn't this the Spiritual Covenant?

So important is Deuteronomy 30:10-16, that it is quoted in part in Romans 10:6-10 as an evidence of Justification through Faith as against that of works to make one righteous, yet Moses used it to show the same thing that Paul showed in Romans, this is the **kainos**/new covenant as in Deuteronomy 30:17,19,20. In Deuteronomy 32:46,47 obedience from the heart is presented as the very **life** of the Israelites, this is indeed the new/**kainos** covenant.

Thus on Mt. Sinai, when God gave the Law to Israel, He in fact gave the Spiritual covenant, but there were symbolic aspects to it, even the symbolic covenant, and the Israelites could not understand because they were yet fleshly (see 2 Corinthians 3:3-16), thus many fell in the wilderness because they were unconverted Hebrews 3:18-19; Hebrews 4:1,2) All this is enough to show that the covenant of Mt. Sinai was both the ceremonial system- the old or symbolic covenant, and the spiritual covenant, later called the **kainos**/new covenant.

THE GIFT OF THE LAW ON TWO TABLES OF STONE

Now, the giving of the Ten Commandments on two tables of stone was also a part of the old covenant, not that this is when the Law came into existence, no it did not, for Cain broke this same Law when he killed Abel (Genesis 4:7,8), God stopped Pharaoh from committing adultery with Abram's wife (Genesis 12: 14-20), and even before Israel reached Mt. Sinai, where the Law was given, the Law with its Sabbath was referred to by God as an imperative for the sons of Israel to keep.

In fact, God rebuked them for not keeping the Law (Exodus 16:22-30). What was the significance of the gift of the Law on Mt. Sinai?

The real significance was how it was given to Israel, it was given to them on two tables of stone.

This was also very symbolical, because the gift of the Law on stone, and written with the finger of God (Exodus 24:12; Exodus 32:15,16), meant the permanent nature of the Law (Psalm 111:7,8), the Law was eternal, thus it was represented as engraved in stones. Another thing the Law written in stones symbolized, was the Law condemning the carnal mind.

The carnal mind was symbolized as stone (Ezekiel 36:26) and since it is not subject to the Law of God (the real problem of sinful man (Romans 8:7)), for the Law to confront this mind is to condemn this mind, and this is exactly what the Law written and engraved in stones meant as seen in 2 Corinthians 3:6,7,9. So we can now say that the Ten Commandments on two tables of literal stone was the symbolic or old covenant/testament.

As long as Israel had the literal Law engraved in stones they had the old covenant, but when the Law on stones was removed from Israel, or their temple, the old covenant was de-emphasized or removed out of the way as such. That the Law was removed from the temple and forever lost is seen in the following statements:

> *"Among the righteous still in Jerusalem to whom had been made plain the divine purpose, were some who determined to place beyond the reach of ruthless hands the sacred ark containing the tables of stone on which had been traced the precepts of the Decalogue. This they did. with mourning and sadness, they secreted the ark in a cave, where it was to be hidden from the people of Israel and Judah because of their sins, and was to be no more restored to them. The sacred ark is yet hidden. It has never*

been disturbed since it was secreted." Ellen G. White, **The Story of Prophets and Kings**, p.453.

"...there are Jewish traditional legends from the Apocrypha which relate that Jeremiah secretly hid the Ark and the alter of incense in a cave...". Grant R. Jeffrey, **Armageddon**, **Appointment with Destiny**, p. 122.

Now that the old covenant (or at least the real symbolical center of it) was hidden away forever, and the old temple of Solomon was burned by the Babylonians (2 Chronicles 36:14-21), seventy years later God instructed the Jews to build a new temple (Ezra 1:2-5), which they finished building (Ezra 6:14-16). What was in the second apartment of this new temple?

Nothing, it was empty, without the ark in which was the Law. Later at the time of the Roman Empire, Pompey, the Roman General found nothing in the second apartment.

> *"He (Josephus) wrote that nothing was found in the Holy of Holies, including the Ark...Most agree the Ark was not in Herod's Temple or in the possession of the Jews at this time".* Doug Wead, David Lewis, and Hal Donaldson, **Where is the Lost Ark**, p. 120

> *"By right of conquest he (Pompey) entered their Temple. It is a fact well known, that he found no image, no statue, no symbolical representation*

of the Deity: the whole presented a naked dome; the sanctuary was unadorned and simple". Roman Historian Tacitus quoted in Thomas Ice and Randall Price, **Ready to Rebuild**, p. 64.

Why was there nothing in the second apartment of the rebuilt temple? Because God Himself had told Jeremiah that He would make a new covenant with the Jews when they returned from Babylonian exile (Jeremiah 31:31-34). This is the same text Paul quoted in Hebrews 8:8-12. Since the center of the Symbolic Covenant was removed, then the things associated with it were to fall into disuse at a gradual pace until they gradually disappeared. With the appearance of Christ on the earth, and at His death, the decay of the Symbolic Covenant speeded up and disappeared altogether at the destruction of Jerusalem by the Romans.

This would mean that the new/**kainos** (qualitatively better) covenant/will had its presentation and emphasis since the return from Babylonian captivity in 536 BCB. How do we know when this new covenant would have its influence? The scriptures tell us. It says:"...the days come..." Jeremiah 31:31. What days? The days "... when I shall bring again their captivity..." (See Jeremiah 31:22-30). And since the Jews became free from Babylonian captivity around 536 BCB (Ezra1:2-6), then from that time the Symbolic Covenant began to decay and the Spiritual Covenant was emphasized.

It was the absence of the ark in which is the Law, it was the absence of the Law on the tables of stone -the real center of the Symbolic Covenant-, and the emphasis on the better covenant that existed alongside with the Symbolic Covenant was made.

One could now understand why God said that the ark of the covenant was no longer to come to the mind of the people when they are given knowledge and understanding, and that Jerusalem-the church-, was to become throne or the ruling place of God (see Jeremiah 3:15-17). One must now ask; that if the law engraved in stones was the old Covenant or the Symbolic Covenant, what was the Spiritual Covenant that was behind it? This is clearly explained in the Bible. It is the Law engraved in the heart (Jeremiah 31:33).

In 2 Corinthians 3 the contrast between the Law engraved in stones, and the Law engraved in the fleshly tables of the heart is presented. 2 Corinthians 3:3-11 shows that the new (**kainos**) covenant is the gift of the Spirit of Life in the heart as against the Law on stones which could only serve to condemn.

The fact that the Law on stones symbolizes the Law of God confronting the stony heart, and that such a thing could only lead to condemnation (Romans 8:7), is what 2 Corinthians 3:6,7,9 is all about, and the gift of the Spirit is the new (**kainos**, qualitatively better) covenant (2 Corinthians 3:3,6,8,9).

But we must have a caution here, we must understand that the Law itself was not the old covenant, the Law engraved in stones-that is, the tables of stone with the Law, that which was mere stones with writings, that was the old covenant. And it would be absurd for God to just have an instrument of condemnation before the Israelites if He loved them and wanted to save them.

But the facts are, that alongside the Law in stones was also the Spiritual Covenant which is the Law in the heart to whosoever repented.

This new (**kainos**, qualitatively better) covenant is seen in Deuteronomy 6:4,5, which is love to God, (see also Deuteronomy 10:12,13), and love to man (Deuteronomy 10:18,19). That this could only be done by a changed heart, a new mind, is seen by the real meaning-the spiritual meaning of circumcision (Deuteronomy 10:16; Deuteronomy 30:6).

Thus the Spiritual Covenant was available to the Israelites in First Witness (OT) times, but the problem with them was that they were full of unbelief (Hebrews 3:7-19, Hebrews 4:1-3), and as the vail of flesh (Hebrews 10:20) was upon their minds they could not see the real purpose of the Law in stones, and this is what 2 Corinthians 3:13-16 is all about.

All these facts are authenticated by what is said in Galatians 3. What was the purpose of the Law (that is, the Law in stones and all the ceremonies, the Symbolic covenant)? It was added (or put towards the Israelites) till Christ should come, and it was a school master, or childhood-guardian to lead us to Christ who embodies the real Spiritual Covenant (Galatians 3:19,24).

Thus the Symbolic Covenant was to point us to the Spiritual Covenant which is Christ the Truth in essence (John 14:6), that we would be justified by the Faith of Jesus Christ (Galatians 2:16, Galatians 3:24), that Faith that was in the ancient prophets (see Hebrews 11 and 1 Peter 1:10,11). We who are of the Faith of Abraham and are thus justified by that Faith are Abraham's sociological and spiritual children (Galatians 3:7).

Therefore the promises in the Covenant/Will are to us, so that the Law engraved in stones, given at Mt. Sinai, could not, and were **never** meant to destroy these true spiritual promises (Galatians 3:17). Also, God never meant that the Law engraved in stones was to be kept by one's own personal initiative in an effort by works to bring oneself into the experience of salvation, a thing that can only be achieved through Faith. God wants us to live in the Law (Galatians 3:12), and according to the principle of "mutual in-ness" (John 15:4,5,7).

This means that the Law must be first placed in our hearts, and this is the new/**kainos** covenant of Hebrews 8:8-13. Thus being in the Law is the Law being in us, and isn't that the same teaching of Deuteronomy 11:1,13, 18,22?

Any obedience to the works of the law that was done as our works righteousness (Deuteronomy 6:24,25) were to be done from a heart full of Faith (Romans 3:28,30,31).

This is why God wished at the time of Mt. Sinai that the Israelites would have "...such an heart in them (to)...keep all (His) commandments..." Deuteronomy 5:29. All these things firmly establish the fact that **the Spiritual Covenant always existed alongside the Symbolic Covenant and was the superior of the two**. When men were saved, it was always by the Spiritual Covenant, never by the symbolic one, and the Symbolic Covenant was always an indicator to the Spiritual Covenant.

That the Spiritual or new/**kainos** (qualitatively better) covenant was existent in the time of the First Witness (OT) can be seen from this: In Romans 8:6 we see that to be Spiritually minded is "life and peace", truly this is the Spiritual or new Covenant; but in Malachi 2:5 God says: "My covenant was with him of life and peace, and I gave them to him..." Surely this is not the old covenant, it is the new/**kainos** or better one, and behold it was in First Witness (OT) times.

All these serve to show us that the anti-nomian idea of covenant theology is wrong, because it makes two ways of salvation at different times, and it robs a whole dispensation (as they call it) of real salvation, since they had to wait for Christ to come. Furthermore, it replaces the Law with Love instead of showing that the Law **is LOVE**; it tells us that the Law is abolished, and it means that obedience of the Law is abolished. But all these things are wrong, because the Law as it is in reality-God's Nature of Love-is not the Old Covenant, neither also is obedience to the Law. The tables of stone, that and all the ceremonial laws were the old or passing away covenant.

OLD (PALAIOS) WILL/COVENANT	NEW (NEOS) WILL/COVENANT	NEW (KAINOS) WILL/COVENANT
1. Holidays/Feasts 2. Rituals 3. Levitical Symbols 4. The tables of Stone with the Law written on it.	1. Incarnation. 2. Life of Jesus 3. Death and Resurrection.	1. Incarnation. 2. Life of Jesus. 3. Death and Resurrection. 4. Ministration in the Heavenly Sanctuary. 5. Spiritual Law. 6. Law in heart. 7. Sanctification. 8. Gift of the Spirit. 9. God being our God, we being His people. 10. The blotting out of sins.

ABOUT THE AUTHOR

NYRON MEDINA is a modern day Christian Reformer and founding Minister of the Thusia Seventh day Adventist Church in Trinidad and Tobago and its sister churches globally.

He was used by YHWH God since the early 1980s to rediscover the authentic understanding of the Gospel as taught by earlier reformers such as German Martin Luther.

His discipline over the years in learning spiritual truths in the school of Christ has provided great leadership as the repairer of the breach that had been caused by years of apostasy from original Seventh day Adventism and ancient Apostolic Christianity.

His leadership has also served as the restorer of the paths to dwell in, linking us today like a golden chain back to the retrieval of the pure biblical truths of the Gospel of Jesus Christ.

No other contemporary Theologian has so accurately recaptured the Gospel, making our church the inheritors of the Reformation and establishing Brother Medina's place in the line of Reformers since the 16th century.

Brother Medina is a prolific writer of Christian religious books, booklets and tracts, long time host and producer, with his wife Sis. Dell Medina, of the Television and Radio programs "Escape for thy Life", which are aired in Trinidad and Tobago and St. Vincent and the Grenadines in the Southern and Eastern Caribbean respectively.

To contact this author call the number **1-868-373-6108**. To learn more about the Thusia Seventh day Adventist Church and receive our **FREE** religious booklets, tracts, video and audio bible studies, call us at Telephone # **1-868-625-0446** or visit our website -www.thusiasdaevangel.com. You may also visit our Church's YouTube channel at **Thusia SDA Gospel**. May God bless you with sinfreeness as you study His words in these last days.

OTHER PUBLICATIONS BY NYRON MEDINA

1. Systematic Theology: The Seven Pillars, The Plan of Salvation.

2. Are Evangelicals True Born Again Christians?

3. An Exposition of Revelation Chapter 13

4. Studies in Pantheism Part 1

5. Studies in Pantheism Part 2

6. Reformation Studies

7. Lucifertheism

8. Studies on Faith

Please contact the Thusia Seventh Day Adventist Church at **Telephone *1-868-625-0446*** for further information on these and other publications.

NOTES

NOTES

Made in United States
Orlando, FL
08 November 2022

24333428R00052